Executive Summary

Expeditionary Warrior 2012 (EW12) was the latest iteration of the Marine Corps' Title 10 wargame. The game, set in a fictional scenario in 2024 Africa, is intended to serve as a means to identify potential gaps and opportunities for enabling joint force access and entry against capable adversaries in an anti-access, area-denial environment. The game was able to explore operational challenges, potential shortfalls and naval integration opportunities for the Joint Operational Access Concept (JOAC), the Navy and Air Force's Air-Sea Battle Concept and conceptual initiatives from the Marine Corps Amphibious Capabilities Working Group.

Key Observations

- There is a need to reconcile Marine Corps operational doctrines with Navy operational doctrines in order to achieve coherence on naval doctrine for achieving joint operational access and the conduct of Single Naval Battle. This includes reconciliation between the Navy's Composite Warfare Concept and the Marine Corps' Operational Maneuver from the Sea and Ship-to-Objective Maneuver.

- The potential need for the ability to rapidly aggregate; the complexities of integrating advance forces operations with Special Operations Forces (SOF), cyber, information and other joint capabilities; and the extensive dialogue over use of particular battlespace coordination measures suggest further analysis for organization of the battlespace and command relationships in a dynamic A2/AD environment is needed.

- Interoperability challenges exist between Navy, Marine Corps and SOF. Capability for littoral reconnaissance, essential for gaining operational access and entry in coastal regions, is lacking. Command relationships between Marine forces, naval component commanders and SOF commanders need to be discussed and clarified.

- Operational issues pertaining to airspace command-and-control and joint effects (kinetic and non-kinetic) integration require further examination.

- Challenges in information fusion and sharing, the existence of multiple non-complementary systems, combined with communication space and bandwidth capacity limitations, impact shared situational awareness.

- Potential capacity shortfalls associated with moving and sustaining support for joint operational access operations exist. Material shortfalls include insufficient surface connectors, support personnel and lift. There is also a need to review and reconcile multiple seabasing concepts to develop an integrated seabasing concept document.

- Cyber capabilities in 2024 will likely be significantly different than those of today. Policy, capability and capacity issues related to cyber will require additional research.

Recommendations

A detailed analysis of discussions and insights conducted during and after EW12 resulted in a number of recommendations to address gaps in command arrangements, SOF interoperability/integration, capacity limitations, information sharing and cyber operations. Some reinforce ongoing Service efforts, while others are new actions for consideration. The major ones include:

Command Arrangements

- Develop a concept for naval (both Navy and Marine Corps) command arrangements.
- Establish a Naval Staff Training Program (NSTP) for Navy and Marine Corps officers.

Navy, Marine Corps and SOF Interoperability and Integration

- Formalize interoperability through a multi-service concept.

Capacity Limitations

- Develop an integrated, cohesive seabasing doctrine that considers the roles and responsibilities of the Maritime Prepositioning Force, Joint Logistics Over the Shore, seabasing, and other Services' afloat prepositioning capabilities.

Information Sharing

- Identify (1) policies that preclude the sharing of data and information; (2) a common set of data standards that enables multiple systems to present information that can be acted upon; and (3) an optimal way to present actionable information that is derived from multiple data feeds in an effort to mitigate the impacts of information overload.

Cyber Operations

- Develop a Service concept for combined arms and capabilities integration.
- Develop architecture, payloads and operational organizations in accordance with the MAGTF Electronic Warfare Concept.

Way Ahead

EW12 will inform a number of approaching experiments, exercises and wargames. These include the Naval Services Game 2012 in September 2012 at the Naval War College; Enhanced MAGTF Operations Limited Objective Experiment 3 during Exercise Dawn Blitz 2013 in June 2013; and EMO Advanced Warfighting Experiment during Exercise Rim of the Pacific 2014, scheduled for the 4th quarter of FY14 in Hawaii.

Table of Contents

Table of Figures

Introduction

This report provides observations and insights from Expeditionary Warrior 2012 (EW12), the latest iteration of the Marine Corps' Title 10 wargame.

The EW series serves as a responsive means to examine operational concepts and future capability requirements for the senior leadership of the Marine Corps. Following up on EW11's initial examination of the Joint Operational Access Concept (JOAC), EW12 sought to further identify potential gaps and opportunities that would enable joint force access to required operational areas against capable adversaries in an anti-access, area-denial (A2/AD) environment.

As a global power, the United States must be able to project military power into any region of the world in support of its strategic interests. Over the past several decades, the United States has been able to deploy forces to an operational area virtually unopposed – from the free flow of personnel and supplies to Korea, Vietnam, Desert Storm, and more recently, to the unchallenged deployment of forces and equipment to Afghanistan in support of Operation Enduring Freedom in 2001 and Kuwait for Operation Iraqi Freedom in 2003.

However, current and future operating environments are increasingly characterized by complexity, uncertainty and rapid change. The dramatic improvement and proliferation of A2/AD capabilities by determined adversaries, enhanced by ready access to the information environment, could challenge U.S. and coalition forces' ability to gain operational access to global areas of interest in the future. Enemies may include states with regional aspirations or non-state/transnational hybrid adversaries that combine high-tech A2/AD resources with low-tech but innovative methods of employment. These opponents could possess a range of conventional and unconventional capabilities – from sophisticated long- and short-range precision weapons, integrated air defenses, electronic warfare and cyber weapons to distributed forces employing combinations of mines, small boats and small arms.

In view of these potential challenges, the Commandant of the Marine Corps (CMC) and the Deputy Commandant, Combat Development and Integration (DC CD&I) directed that EW12 examine

> **Anti-access**: Those actions and capabilities, usually long-range, designed to prevent an opposing force from entering an operational area.
>
> **Area-denial**: Those actions and capabilities, usually of shorter-range, designed not to keep an opposing force out, but to limit its freedom of action within the operational area.
>
> *Joint Operational Access Concept,*
> 17 January 2012

capabilities associated with gaining and maintaining operational access to global regions against capable, dynamic adversaries. This report, which provides observations and recommendations from EW12, is broadly divided into five sections. The first part of the report is an introduction to A2/AD, its challenges to the joint force and EW's role in examining these challenges. The second section is a description of the wargame, its methodology and the scenario. The third and fourth sections provide key observations from the wargame followed by a detailed discussion on the issues and problems related to each of these observations. The final section outlines potential solutions to these issues, suggests actionable tasks for stakeholders, and presents a way ahead for how EW12 outputs can inform future experiments, exercises, concept development and other wargames.

A2/AD and Implications for the Joint Force

EW12's sponsor organization, DC CD&I G-3/G-5, made the wargame a venue to further examine the application of ongoing joint and Marine Corps concepts and initiatives in the A2/AD environment. These include, but are not limited to:

- The Joint Operational Access Concept (JOAC). In 2011, the EW11 wargame served as a mechanism to inform the JOAC. The concept, which describes in broad terms the joint approach for overcoming A2/AD challenges, posits cross-domain synergy, a complementary employment of capabilities in different domains such that each enhances the effectiveness and compensates for the vulnerabilities of the others, which will allow the joint force to have greater freedom of action.   The JOAC was signed by the Chairman of the Joint Chiefs of Staff in January 2012.

- Air-Sea Battle, or ASB, a concept unveiled by the Marine Corps, Navy and Air Force in 2011, was developed as a way of gaining and maintaining operational access primarily via the two services' strike capabilities (kinetic, cyber and electronic). The concept centers on networked, integrated attack-in-depth to disrupt, destroy and defeat A2/AD threats. Air-naval forces would be organized by mission and networked for integrated operations across all the domains – maritime, air, land, space and the information environment, which includes cyberspace.[1] This tight integration would create a synergy in which one's capabilities could enable the other's mission-critical activities.

- Outputs from the Amphibious Capabilities Working Group (ACWG) – directed by CMC in September 2011 to review the strategic role, operating concepts and naval integration of the Marine Corps and the amphibious force – validated that amphibious operations will continue to be a valuable military capability, but postulated that the new operating

---

[1] "The Air-Sea Battle Summary Concept Summary," HQMC Air-Sea Battle Office, 10 November 2011, http://www.marines.mil/unit/hqmc/Pages/TheAir-SeaBattleconceptsummary.aspx.

environment will require significant adaptation and the establishment of a unified Navy-Marine Corps approach to organization, programs, training, exercises and operating principles.[2]

EW12 was designed to examine the application of these concepts with current and future Marine Corps capabilities operating in a joint context against capable conventional and unconventional adversaries. Although EW12 planners recognize the importance of diplomatic, informational and economic factors in the strategic and operational calculus of any conflict, the primary focus of this wargame was on military operations.

In the design of EW12, planners considered several factors that impact joint military operations in the A2/AD environment. First, an adversary's strategy of protraction through A2/AD may increase risk to the joint force, influence decision-making, and potentially restrict maneuver and operational tempo. In EW12, the adversary's protracted use of capable air, surface and sub-surface assets over an extended period could increase operational risks for the joint and combined force. Persistence of these threats may further limit friendly force operational tempo and its ability to maneuver in the battlespace. As such, future joint forces would need to adopt a mindset to overwhelm, mitigate or neutralize A2/AD threats to reduce operational risk and enhance freedom of maneuver.

Second, the naval force provides operational tempo and maneuver and facilitates follow-on operations for the joint force. This is the vision implied in Single Naval Battle (SNB)[3] and as articulated by the ACWG. However, the application of SNB would require a paradigm shift in command arrangements, battlespace organization and information sharing. As a result, the wargame was designed to feature a combined joint task force (CJTF) formed to address a regional crisis in 2024, with the preponderance of naval forces setting the conditions for Phases I and II. These forces aggregated upon arrival into the CJTF joint operations area (JOA) from the Continental United States (CONUS) and forward deployed from other GCC areas of responsibility (AORs) without time to integrate prior to conducting operations. Efficient and effective integration of Navy and Marine Corps forces would need to be a factor critical in crisis response operations.

---

[2] MROC Decision Memorandum 17-2012.

[3] *Naval Amphibious Capability in the 21ˢᵗ Century: Strategic Opportunity and a Vision for Change – Report of the Amphibious Capabilities Working Group*, 27 April 2012, p. 34: "A single naval battle approach views the maritime domain as an indivisible whole, allowing us to express the actions and forces within it as inherently integrated in effect. It provides a unifying perspective for naval operations and bridges the seams between air, land, and sea. It allows the commander to effectively focus the effort of all elements of the naval force in the greater context of the joint operation."

Third, in A2/AD environments, the joint force succeeds through relative overmatch, but this overmatch requires time to organize and may require a lodgment to be secured. Friendly forces need to establish a relative advantage over the enemy in capability and capacity. In addition to capabilities, participants expressed concern about sufficient capacity for assets such as mine countermeasures (MCM), amphibious lift, command and control (C2), bandwidth, and throughput. Joint forces must be capable of gaining and maintaining access while deploying from home stations, while en route to forward areas, and during employment throughout the AO. EW12 was designed to examine expected access challenges with the required capabilities and forces in order to gain, build and defend lodgments to support follow-on operations.

EW12 Approach, Objectives, Focus Areas and Methodology

EW12 employed a battle-study approach that established a campaign plan prior to execution of the Main Event. This approach steered game participants toward substantive discussion that led to actionable issues vice creation of a concept of operations. This methodology was supplemented by an expert A2/AD panel, guest speakers and technical briefs, and facilitated an opportunity to focus on the issues rather than force-on-force planning.

EW12 Special Events

A2/AD Panelists
LtGen Chip Gregson (Ret), USMC; RADM Terry Kraft, USN; RADM Brad Hicks, USN (Ret); and Dr. Scott Truver

Capabilities Briefs
Joint Logistics Over the Shore – LtCol Paul "Dutch" Bertholf, USMC, J-4, The Joint Staff
Seabasing – Mr. Jim Strock, Seabasing Integration Division, CD&I, HQMC

Guest Speaker
Gen James N. Mattis, USMC, Commander, U.S. Central Command – *The Future of Joint Force Crisis Response and Power Projection*

The EW12 Main Event occurred on 5-9 March 2012 at The Westin Hotel in Washington, D.C., following 10 months of conferences, workshops and planning events. It featured 200 participants and guests representing all five Services of the U.S. Armed Forces, the Joint Staff, Office of the Secretary of Defense, U.S. Central Command, U.S. Special Operations Command and 14 partner nations.

EW12 was not designed as a quantitative, model-driven event focused on analysis and comparison of alternatives between specific systems and technologies. Rather, the Main Event was a seminar-style wargame focused on examining Marine Corps and naval concepts and identifying broad capability challenges associated with gaining and maintaining joint operational access in a 2024 environment. Senior Marine Corps leadership approved the following as the overall game objective:

- Identify gaps and opportunities in joint and service capabilities required to gain joint force access and entry, and conduct follow-on operations when opposed by tactically unconventional and conventional adversaries.

Nested under the overall objective of the game were five sub-objectives, which were products of friction points uncovered during planning for the wargame. The EW12 <u>sub-objectives</u> were:

- Aggregation of Combined Forces Maritime Component Commander (CFMCC) sea control and power projection forces.
- Interoperability of Special Operations Forces (SOF) and CFMCC lead elements.
- Overcoming A2/AD challenges to achieving entry.
- Establish functional joint lodgment in an area with austere infrastructure.
- CFMCC use of sea control and power projection in support of follow-on operations.

EW12's focus areas were culled from initial findings of the ACWG. Research questions were, in turn, linked to the sub-objectives and focus areas in order to focus participants' discussions. The EW12 <u>focus areas</u> were:

- Single Naval Battle
- Littoral Mobility
- Littoral Maneuver
- Aviation Deployment Concepts
- Force Aggregation
- Amphibious Doctrine

- Cyber Operations
- Operationalize the Seabase
- Command Relationships
- Logistics Over the Shore
- Expeditionary Mobility
- Maritime Prepositioning

The wargame consisted of three moves containing a total of five vignettes. Across the three moves, these vignettes focused participants' attention on research questions linked to the sub-objectives and focus areas. Wargame participants were organized into four blue cells that reviewed an identical slate of research questions. The cells were led by Marine, Navy and coalition leadership and consisted of a variety of subject-matter experts (SMEs) across all the domains. One of the cells had over 50% multinational officers, providing a broader, coalition perspective to the issues. The red cell, with members embedded in each blue cell, provided the enemy's perspective on participant discussions – rather than testing Blue Force planning efforts as part of a move/counter-move construct.

At the end of each game move, a plenary session was held and each cell briefed and discussed their top insights. These plenary meetings allowed participants to synthesize the four cells' outputs and provided the game's flag-level leadership an opportunity to contribute to a holistic dialogue. On the final day of the Main Event, participants were reorganized into groups of different composition to assess EW12 by warfighting function: command and control (C2)/command relationships, fires/intelligence, maneuver/force protection, and logistics. This created an additional venue to further synthesize observations made during cell and plenary discussions.

Classified Excursion

Although the EW12 Main Event was unclassified to allow involvement from a wide spectrum of participants, discussions regarding many of the competing A2/AD systems could only occur at the classified level. Therefore, a classified excursion was conducted to ensure feasibility of the EW12 CONOPS and identify any new joint/Marine Corps capability gaps. In February 2012, prior to the EW12 Main Event, 58 SMEs spanning all domains gathered for a classified excursion to conduct detailed SECRET-level discussions about friendly force platform capabilities and the enemy threats in the EW12 scenario. The following A2/AD threats described in the JOAC were assessed:

- Ballistic and Cruise Missiles (B/CM)
- C2 and Electromagnetic (C2/EM) Spectrum
- Cyber and Information Operations (IO)
- Precision-Guided Rockets, Artillery, Mortars and Missiles (G-RAMM)
- Surface, Sub-Surface and Mine Warfare
- Intelligence, Surveillance and Reconnaissance (ISR)
- Fixed- and Rotary-Wing (FW/RW) Aviation
- Space/Counter-Space Operations

Assessments of these threats were made against the EW12 CJTF CONOPS, producing a list of assumptions about the A2/AD threats in the scenario that served as a baseline for discussions at the wargame.[4]

Scenario

EW12 used a fictional scenario set in 2024 West Africa, featuring adversaries that mirror likely future threats that possess capabilities robust enough to challenge an intervening joint force. At the center of the scenario was a politically unstable allied nation – Savanna – with an internal irregular enemy, the Free Savanna Movement (FSM). An invading neighbor, the West

---

[4] *EW12 Classified Excursion – Unclassified Assumptions and Injects*, 28 February 2012, provides an unclassified look at the methodology used to assess EW12's A2/AD threats. A SECRET-level report about the EW12 Classified Excursion can be found on the SIPRNET:
http://www.mccdc.usmc.smil.mil/g35_repository/EW12%20Classified%20Excursion/.

African Federation (WAF), provided a conventional enemy, while a regional power, Volta, supported the adversaries against intervention by a U.S.-led coalition.

The scenario featured conventional and unconventional adversaries armed with credible A2/AD capabilities – surface-to-surface ballistic missiles (SSBMs), anti-ship cruise missiles (ASCMs), integrated air defense systems (IADS), small boats and submarines – in order to present a viable anti-access challenge. WAF also possessed a large multi-corps ground force capable of invasion into Savanna. Geography for the scenario consisted of complex terrain including rivers, poor infrastructure and a large coastal population center. Central to player debate were the Savanna Islands, located roughly 600 kilometers west of Savanna, which provided potential air and sea ports of debarkation (APODs/SPODs) for the advancing CJTF.

The fictional conflict depicted in EW12 began when FSM, with assistance from WAF, a neighboring state with regional aspirations, initiated attacks to overthrow the Savanna government.WAF also took advantage of Savanna's internal instability to initiate a ground invasion into Savanna. The United Nations Security Council

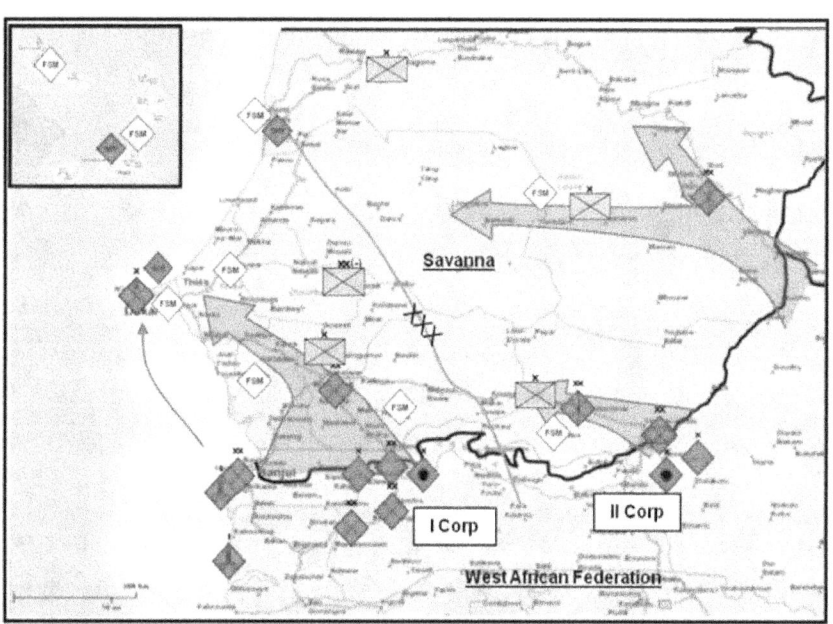

Figure 1. Enemy ground threat situation.

passed a resolution authorizing the use of force to re-establish the territorial integrity of Savanna and neutralize WAF's offensive capability. The mission statement for the U.S.-led coalition CJTF Savanna was:

- When directed, CJTF Savanna will conduct Operation RESTORE SOVEREIGNTY to re-establish the territorial integrity of Savanna, neutralize WAF's offensive capability and transition security responsibilities to U.N. forces.

Game Moves and Vignette Structure

Wargame planners developed a five-phase campaign for CJTF Savanna. Of these five, only the first three were played in EW12: Phase I – Achieve Access, Phase II – Gain Entry and Phase III – Follow-on Operations. While considered important, the remaining phases, stability operations and the transition to U.N. operations, fell outside the game's overall objective. Vignettes within each move were designed to give EW12 participants opportunities to more closely examine specific sections of the CJTF CONOPS and focus discussions on the game's sub-objectives and focus areas. Because the campaign plan had been completed prior to the start of the Main Event, participants were able to free themselves from a crisis action planning process and concentrate on the conceptual, doctrinal and capability issues central to each game move.

Move 1 – Phase I: Achieve Access / Setting Conditions

Move 1 coincided with Phase I, when the joint force objectives were to neutralize A2/AD capabilities, gain maritime and air superiority, protect and reinforce Savanna government forces, seize advance bases in the Savanna Islands, and set the conditions for entry operations into Savanna.

- **Vignette 1 – Savanna Islands Anti-Access:** The first vignette highlighted CFMCC concepts, capabilities and doctrine in an anti-access environment. Players were asked whether the lead elements of the CFMCC (a carrier strike group (CSG) and amphibious ready group/Marine expeditionary unit (ARG/MEU)) had sufficient capabilities to accomplish their missions, if solutions or resources existed to address potential capability gaps, and to examine alternates to maneuver to mitigate anti-access threats. Players also addressed critical capabilities needed to maintain missile defense against the enemy's conventional anti-access threats.

- **Vignette 2 – Interoperability of SOF and CFMCC Lead Elements:** The second vignette shifted the spotlight to interoperability issues between SOF and CFMCC lead elements. In the context of the scenario, participants discussed ways that the CFMCC and CFSOCC could mutually support each other through augmentation and liaison. In particular, players debated the roles and responsibilities of in-theater SOF for maritime advance force operations, a key enabler for the CJTF's landing force operations.

Move 2 – Phase II: Gain Entry

Phase II highlighted the CJTF's forcible entry efforts. Key tasks were the seizure of a lodgment, the rapid introduction of joint and combined forces, an attack to secure the city of Touba, and the continued expansion of APODs and SPODs in the Savanna Islands.

- **Vignette 3 – Area-Denial Challenges:** The third vignette examined the enemy's area-denial capabilities that posed the greatest risk to mission accomplishment. Players discussed interoperability gaps that exist in joint and service capabilities and doctrine for C2, command arrangements, and methods for the CFMCC to maintain maritime superiority against an attack on the seabase and lodgment. Additionally, players detailed doctrinal changes that needed to occur if the MAGTF C2 remained afloat, as well as the impacts on airspace and fires coordination if MAGTF aviation remained afloat while MAGTF C2 transitioned ashore.

- **Vignette 4 – Joint Lodgment:** The fourth vignette focused participants on the joint lodgment in the Savanna Islands and a seabase to facilitate follow-on operations ashore in Savanna. Operations revolve around repairs and improvements at the APODs/SPODs, Joint Logistics Over the Shore (JLOTS) and the flow of forces through APODs/SPODs. Players discussed challenges relating to throughput, optimal force flow for key enablers, requirements to expand APODs for joint operations and the competition between amphibious shipping, MPF and JLOTS for connectors.

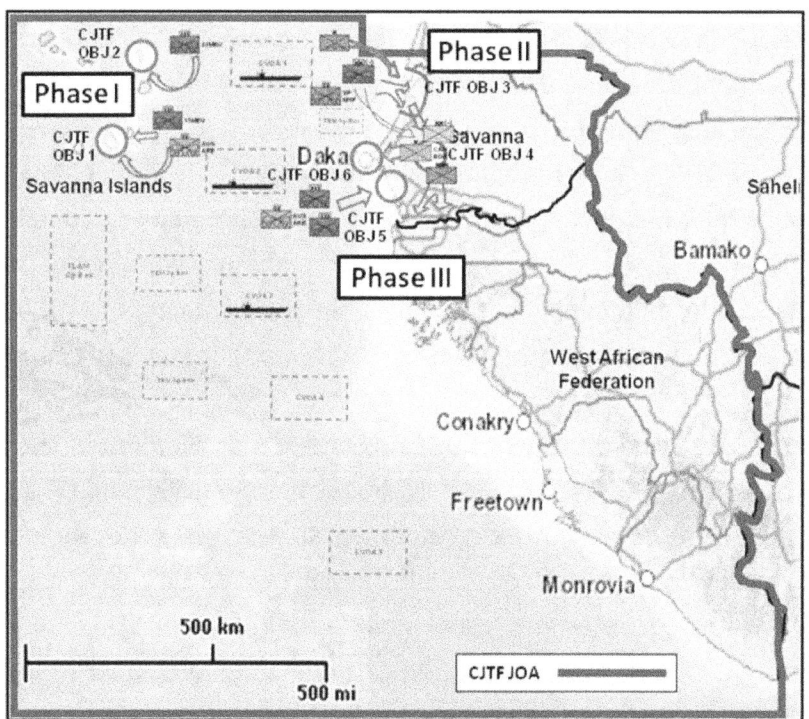

Figure 2. CJTF Concept of Operations, Phases I-III.

Move 3 – Phase III: Follow-on Operations

Move 3 focused player discussions around Phase –III – CFMCC Activities to Support Follow-on Operations. The CFMCC worked to isolate the enemy-held capital city of Dakar in order to facilitate Savanna forces' re-taking of the city and begin preparations for transitioning the battlespace for extended ground operations.

- **Vignette 5 – CFMCC Support to Follow-on Operations:** The fifth vignette focused on battlespace management issues for the CFMCC while supporting decisive CFLCC operations. Participants discussed methods and doctrine that could be applied toward CFMCC control of landward battlespace, including the Maritime Operations Center (MOC). They also addressed seams created by the traditional application of functional componency and geographic domains during joint operations in the littorals.

Key Observations

Gaining and maintaining operational access in the face of armed opposition involves two conceptually distinct elements. First, the joint force must be able to overcome the adversary's anti-access and area-denial capabilities through the application of combat power. Second, maintaining access requires the joint force to move and support the necessary combat power over the required distances.[5] EW12 was able to examine aspects of both of these issues. Key observations include:

- There is a need to reconcile Marine Corps operational doctrines with Navy operational doctrines in order to achieve coherence on naval doctrine for achieving joint operational access and the conduct of SNB.
- The potential need for the ability to rapidly aggregate forces; the complexities of integrating advance forces operations with SOF, cyber, information and other joint capabilities; and the extensive dialogue over use of particular battlespace coordination measures suggest further analysis for organization of the battlespace and command relationships in a dynamic A2/AD environment is needed.
- Interoperability challenges exist between Navy, Marine Corps and SOF. Capability for littoral reconnaissance, essential for gaining operational access and entry in coastal regions, is lacking. Command relationships between Marine forces, naval component commanders and SOF commanders need to be discussed and clarified.
- Operational issues pertaining to airspace command-and-control and joint effects (kinetic and non-kinetic) integration require further examination.
- Challenges in information fusion and sharing, the existence of multiple non-complementary systems, combined with communication space and bandwidth capacity limitations, impact shared situational awareness.

---

[5] *Joint Operational Access Concept*, 17 January 2012, p. 5.

- Potential capacity shortfalls associated with moving and sustaining support for joint operational access operations exist. Materiel shortfalls include insufficient surface connectors and lift. There is also a need to review and reconcile multiple seabasing concepts to develop an integrated seabasing concept document.
- Cyber capabilities in 2024 will likely be significantly different than those of today. Policy, capability and capacity issues related to cyber will require additional research.

Supporting Discussions

There is a need to reconcile Marine Corps operational doctrines with Navy operational doctrines in order to achieve coherence on naval doctrine for achieving joint operational access and the conduct of a Single Naval Battle.
At EW12, players discussed how differences in approach between the Navy's Composite Warfare Commander (CWC) concept and the Marine Corps' Ship-to-Objective Maneuver (STOM) and Operational Maneuver from the Sea (OMFTS) concepts could hamper coherence while planning for operational access and entry.

Over the past few decades, the maritime environment has changed significantly due to increasingly complex shipboard systems, proliferation of more capable, longer range weapons, and the vast amount and rapid flow of data / information required for decision-making. The Navy developed the CWC concept as a way for an officer in tactical charge (OTC) to maintain unity of command of a naval force – regardless of its size or composition while decentralizing execution through the use of subordinate commanders responsible for a particular environment (e.g., air, surface, sub-surface) or function (antiair, antisubmarine, anti-surface or strike). Officers also may be designated coordinators of types of assets within the force (e.g., air element coordinator). An important distinction between CWC commanders and coordinators is that warfare commanders would have tactical control over assigned resources and may initiate actions themselves based on the CWC's guidance (akin to mission-type orders), but coordinators would only be allowed to execute policy and could not act independently.[6] Other concept and capability developments, such as the Aegis fire control system, Littoral Combat Ships (LCS) and Cooperative Engagement Capability (CEC)[7], further evolved naval capabilities, but with little change to the CWC concept.

---

[6] *NWP 3-56 Composite Warfare Doctrine*, September 2010, Chs. 1 and 2.
[7] Cooperative Engagement Capability (CEC) is a real-time sensor netting system that enables high quality situational awareness and integrated fire control capability. CEC is designed to enhance the antiair warfare (AAW) capability of ships and aircraft by the netting of battle force sensors to provide a single, distributed AAW defense capability. CEC enables integrated fire control to counter increasingly capable cruise missiles and manned aircraft. U.S. Navy Fact File, 18 November 2011, http://www.navy.mil/navydata/fact_display.asp?cid=2100&tid=325&ct=2.

> **Modern threats call for the integrated application of naval capabilities in the maritime domain and beyond.**

Maneuver warfare has shaped contemporary Marine Corps thinking in the same way that CWC has shaped the Navy's approach to warfighting. Published in 1996, OMFTS attempted to apply the maneuver warfare vision to amphibious operations in the 21st century environment. OMFTS focuses thinking on the operational objective; uses the sea as maneuver space; generates overwhelming tempo and momentum; pits strength against weakness; emphasizes intelligence, deceptions and flexibility; and integrates all organic, joint and combined assets.[8] STOM, written in 1997 and updated in 2011, describes the method by which OMFTS is realized – assaults conducted from over-the-horizon to reach objectives deep inland.

Working group discussions focused on the attributes and differences between CWC and OMFTS/STOM. The former is marked by meticulous coordination of environments across domains and functions that creates a "bubble" to provide for the defense of the force and supports sea control. The latter philosophy – OMFTS/STOM – advocates bold maneuver to reach deep-inland objectives, suggesting an offensive mindset and an orientation toward power projection. These different approaches, and the processes and mechanisms used to execute them, while appropriate for each individual service, have not been reconciled with each other. EW12 players also were unable to reconcile the two different approaches to warfighting in the Savanna littorals.

Aside from the differences in conceptual approaches, discussion also examined potential duplication or distinctions in the roles and responsibilities for various designated individuals / commanders in executing joint operational access and entry operations. For example, the CWC may designate an amphibious warfare commander (AWC) whose responsibilities can duplicate some of the duties of the Commander, Amphibious Task Force (CATF), but who may not be the CATF. Doctrine does not provide any guidance on how to reconcile these potential differences in authority and responsibility between different AWC/CATF.

Modern threats call for the integrated application of *naval* capabilities in the maritime domain and beyond. Navy and Marine Corps capabilities and expertise need to be focused on the entirety of the operational area. Navy and Marine Corps doctrine should be reviewed to ensure

---

[8] *Operational Maneuver from the Sea*, 1996.

they are complementary, consistent, coherent and capable of supporting joint operating access and entry requirements.

The potential need for the ability to rapidly aggregate forces; the complexities of integrating advance forces operations with Special Operations Forces (SOF), cyber, information and other joint capabilities; and the extensive dialogue over use of particular battlespace coordination measures (e.g., Amphibious Objective Area (AOA) and the High-Density Airspace Control Zone (HIDACZ) suggest further analysis for organization of the battlespace and command relationships in a dynamic A2/AD environment is needed.

One of the main challenges players discussed in EW12 concerned force aggregation. In A2/AD operations, flexibility, responsiveness, and required capabilities needed for specific missions in a dynamic environment may require the joint task force commander to periodically aggregate his forces. Participants in EW12 noted that while the Marine Corps currently has in staffing a concept of employment document that outlines capabilities and limitations of disaggregated ARG/MEU operations, there is not a comparable document that discusses the concept of employment and relationships for the aggregation of a larger force.

Force aggregation could cause numerous second- and third-order effects that could potentially impact the commander's desired operational tempo. Players emphasized that aggregation must consider at-sea transfer limitations. Planners would have to develop options for establishing an intermediate staging base (ISB) for complicated re-arrangement of forces and equipment that could not reasonably be reconfigured for timely at-sea transfer. During EW12, an ISB came with a price – loss of deception and surprise; personnel, SPOD and hardening requirements; and a need for TBMD assets.

This led to discussions about the need for adaptive force packaging, described in the Naval Operating Concept as a bundling of capabilities to address missions across the range of military operations (ROMO).[9] Participants also noted that force aggregation required interoperable information systems – across boundaries set by country, Service, function or domain – to enable a more effective common operating picture (information sharing issues are outlined later in the Supporting Discussions section).

---

[9] "Adaptive force packaging generates the *globally distributed, mission-tailored forces* required to resource the demands of the combatant commanders. The standard CSG and ARG force packages can be scaled up by incorporating additional ships; or disaggregated into smaller surface action groups or individual ships to conduct the full range of military operations, including capacity building, theater security cooperation (TSC) and combat operations." – *Naval Operating Concept 2010: Implementing the Maritime Strategy*, p. 29.

Force aggregation can also refer to meshing across types of forces (SOF or GPF), capabilities, domains and effects (kinetic and non-kinetic). The fire support construct used to conduct planning for non-kinetic effects is a better fit for some lines of operation such as information operations, but continually evolving, complex capabilities like cyber may require a new framework.

EW12 also highlighted the CFMCC's attempts to establish unity of effort and exposed challenges in C2 and battlespace coordination. Participants discussed employment of some combination of the AOA and HIDACZ as ways to organize the battlespace. These options included:

- One AOA extending shallowly inland to cover the ship-to-shore objectives only. Simultaneously establish air routes and HIDACZs within the AOA and other deeper objectives outside the AOA and conduct isolated missions controlled by the CATF or CLF within CFLCC- and CFACC-controlled areas.
- One large AOA extending to deep inland objectives that would be owned by the CATF and CLF. Although the CATF or CLF have the comfort of owning the entire battlespace, battlespace management would become more complex and arduous. Tempo would slow when other components are required to request permission to conduct adjacent operations that affect the AOA.
- Designating AOAs around multiple dispersed amphibious force objectives and linking to each one via air routes. This method could lend itself to surprise and reduce the enemy's ability to focus A2/AD efforts in any one place. However, the amphibious force would not have complete control over the near-areas surrounding the AOAs, which may slow down maneuver if deconfliction is not executed smoothly.
- Establishing multiple air routes and HIDACZs with no defined areas of operation or AOA. The CATF would coordinate with other commanders for accomplishing CFMCC missions scattered across the JOA with no specified amphibious tagline.

EW12 attendees asserted that the tools exist to exercise creativity and ingenuity when planning the dynamic interaction, boundaries and operational command structures. Participants stated that commanders should not think of battlespace in this A2/AD environment as singularly owned. In fact, battlespace is a coordination measure that facilitates C2 and operational flexibility.

Interoperability challenges exist between Navy, Marine Corps and SOF. Capability for littoral reconnaissance, essential for gaining operational access in coastal regions, is lacking.

Command relationships between Marine forces, naval component commanders and SOF commanders need to be discussed and clarified.

At EW12, players discussed how system interoperability challenges disrupt the ability of naval forces to effectively integrate and create closer operational relationships with SOF. SOF are rarely under the control of the maritime component commander, which creates C2 challenges and complicates SOF integration with general purpose forces (GPF). These disconnects could be particularly problematic during advance force operations, which have different meanings to naval and SOF planners. An integrated approach to maritime advance force operations to shape the operational environment for littoral access is needed to close tactical integration and interoperability gaps between SOF and naval forces. EW12 participants were quick to point out that although ad hoc integration at the small unit level exists between naval and SOF units, interoperability challenges across the warfighting functions and institutional roadblocks prevent formalized mutual support and force integration needed at the enterprise level.

> **An integrated approach to maritime advance force operations to shape the operational environment for littoral access is needed to close tactical integration and interoperability gaps between SOF and naval forces.**

Gaps in doctrine, training and education exist in the command arrangements and command relationships among the Navy, Marine Corps and SOF. Doctrine and concepts to address C2 interoperability and integration are either absent or too ambiguous to develop tactics, techniques and procedures for real world operations. The supported/supporting dynamic is often colored by operational philosophies – GPF are generally more comfortable with unity of command to ensure unity of effort in the joint force commander's AO, while SOF seek to maximize operational independence in order to fulfill taskings from a parallel chain of command (e.g., national taskings via the TSOC).[10] Inadequate integrated training between GPF and SOF was reflected in the lack of SOF participation in Exercise Bold Alligator in January-February 2012. GPF and SOF often plan and train separately, under the assumption that they will be operating in different AOs. However, operational realities compel continuous interaction between GPF and SOF.

Additionally, an overall lack of awareness of complementary capabilities reflects a naval and SOF education gap. Marines and SOF are highly complementary and have several similar

---

[10] *JP 3-05 Special Operations*, 18 April 2011, p. III-13, http://www.dtic.mil/doctrine/new_pubs/jp3_05.pdf.

capabilities and characteristics. For example, SOF provide specialized skill sets, precision effects and a global steady state security presence, but their operational effectiveness is constrained by limited forward basing, challenges to access, and ungoverned or contested spaces. Meanwhile, the Navy-Marine Corps team provides forward-deployed platforms, integrated aviation, manpower, firepower, trained staff planners, scalable ground reinforcement and sustainment capabilities.[11] EW12 players noted that it would be problematic for SOF and naval forces to independently meet current and future operational demands without collaboration.

One of the gaps players identified during EW12 centered on naval and SOF perspectives on advance force operations. To Navy and Marine Corps planners, advance force operations focus on enabling landing force operations with mine countermeasures (MCM), hydrographic reconnaissance, seizure of key amphibious force objectives, preliminary bombardment, underwater demolitions and air support.[12] SOF, however, have a broader definition that discusses target-specific operational preparation of the battlespace (OPB) prior to the arrival of the main assault force. In the EW12 scenario, CJTF taskings would likely preoccupy SOF that were already operating in theater as outlined during Vignette 2 of the wargame, underscoring the need for an organic amphibious reconnaissance capability within ARG/MEUs – as reconnaissance Marines were utilized to fill the ranks of the U.S. Marine Corps Forces Special Operations Command (MARSOC).

Operational issues pertaining to airspace command-and-control and joint effects (kinetic and non-kinetic) integration were challenges that require further examination.
EW12 participants wrestled with a variety of approaches to organize the battlespace in an effort to address amphibious landing requirements, ship-to-shore objectives, and interrelated joint fires and operations across all domains. Joint doctrine dictates that all air control and support originating from land, sea or air will be coordinated through the Joint Force Air Component Commander (JFACC), Airspace Control Authority (ACA) and the Area Air Defense Commander (AADC).[13]

Particular to the Marine Corps, the MEB force fires coordination center (FFCC) will work through the aviation combat element's (ACE) tactical air control center (TACC) and tactical air direction center (TADC) for tactical air requests from subordinate fire support coordination centers (FSCC) and any airborne system maneuver and movement employed in the JOA. Joint doctrine governing fires exists, but some wargame participants expressed concern over a naval force's ability to effectively coordinate fires for a force trying to execute STOM. Naval fire

---

[11] ACWG Report, p. 38.
[12] *JP 3-02 Amphibious Operations*, 10 August 2009, p. III-52, GL-6.
[13] *JP-3-09 Joint Fire Support,* 30 June 2010.

support for amphibious operations alone can become complicated. Problems exacerbated with the addition of complex A2/AD threats – including electronic warfare and GPS-denial capabilities – and over-the-horizon standoff distances that stretch proven communication and coordination mechanisms. Fires would have to be provided by alternate means such as Navy and Air Force strike. As the CFMCC prosecutes the amphibious campaign, the CFACC has overall responsibility of the air campaign. CWC, however, delegates the naval force's strike responsibilities to its strike warfare commander. Participants debated which organization would be best positioned to be a single airspace coordinator, and how best to prevent overlapping air domains.

The issues become more complex when unmanned aerial ISR systems, antiair defenses and TBMD capabilities are considered. The CJTF Savanna CONOPS calls for the naval force's Aegis to initially provide TBMD for both the fleet and the Savanna Islands lodgment until Army Patriot and Terminal High-Altitude Air Defense (THAAD) batteries can be established. As additional assets become operational, numerous agencies would be required to continuously deconflict operations as air domains across the components threaten to overlap. Additionally, players described how the Navy's detect-to-engage sequence (for Aegis or otherwise) is optimized for the sea and not land, segregating itself from other systems and Services that are intended to track and engage targets ashore in support of the amphibious operation. Underlying these issues is a knowledge gap due to a lack of practice to jointly conduct fires and airspace coordination, whether by exercising with real forces or by tabletop without troops.

Challenges in information fusion and sharing, the existence of multiple non-complementary systems, combined with communication space and bandwidth capacity limitations, impact shared situational awareness.

The vast amount and speed of information flow in a complex A2/AD environment will make the development of a common operating picture (COP) more difficult. EW12 players were not sure if the COP is a sufficient concept to help manage future information complexity. One reason articulated for this concern was that the COP does not provide enough of a holistic picture of all the activities and events that might affect the CJTF mission. Additionally, ISR assets meant to help develop the COP are numerous, but there is a severe lack of information infrastructure to support the dissemination of information across platforms. An example of this issue is the lack of processes to enable the CSG to push information to the ARG.

The information environment becomes more complex when staffs are deployed aboard ships. Staffs may potentially be distributed across numerous vessels. This poses a physical challenge to information sharing, as staffs may not be able to access information systems in a timely manner due to limited space and bandwidth. Another complicating factor is the aggregation of multiple forces' commands at sea, and the impact this will have on information fusion. Policies and processes will have to provide guidance on how to coordinate efforts of, for example, multiple MEUs forming a MEB regarding fires.

Information fusion for effective joint fires coordination will likely pose another challenge in a complex A2/AD environment. When multiple MEUs are aggregated, planners must consider how the joint targeting process and information dissemination and processes might be different. The issue of information coordination and fusion afloat can also be challenging for the MEU ACE. One potential solution is to decentralize fires authorities to lower-level units that are closer to the fight in an effort to reduce the complexity of the current process and mitigate information coordination issues across distributed staffs.

Players identified the need to develop protocols that will more effectively enable SOF/GPF information sharing. The CFSOCC commander will need to see the larger picture of the fight, and the GPF will need to see CFSOCC's picture. It is unclear if doctrine exists that explains how this information sharing relationship might work. Some participants noted that if there is doctrine, it is poorly understood.

Further complicating the force's ability to share information is the proliferation of non-complementary systems. Players expressed a belief that sequestering information by system instead of by classification acts as a severe drag on tempo. Instead of having information systems that only have one level of classification, these systems need to have the capability to manage multiple classification levels. Systems need to manage the information that users can access based on user identification. The limited space afloat compels the need to maximize the functionality of systems versus proliferating different systems in finite shipboard space.

When the fight features a broader multinational coalition, the need to have a common information sharing system is critical. Players said that during Exercise Bold Alligator 2012, participants leveraged the Combined Enterprise Regional Information Exchange (CENTRIX) system to conduct pre-planning. Because of the current configuration of ships that lack CENTRIX connections, the use of CENTRIX was abandoned during the actual exercise. Liaison officers (LNOs) can serve as one mechanism to share information with coalition militaries, but will be insufficient in an A2/AD scenario because of the limited number of LNOs dealing with a large volume of data to disseminate.

There are additional personal, physical and electronic limitations to information sharing. LNOs may provide a limited means to share information with coalition partners, but the use of LNOs requires personality-driven trust. There is a significant need for senior leadership to articulate more effective policy that will enable information sharing with coalition members on a personal level and via electronic means. The issue of trust and coordination with LNOs also extends to the lack of intelligence sharing among U.S. forces and coalition members. Without effective integration of battlespace intelligence, the development of a COP is severely degraded.

Physically, platforms such as ships can conduct multiple missions, but these platforms cannot do everything simultaneously. Afloat staffs may have access to information sharing systems conduits, but this access is physically limited by the space available to install systems. The lack of shipboard space for multiple information sharing systems further drives the need for new ways to sequester information of differing classification levels within systems.

Electronically, there is a range of challenges from bandwidth, information assurance and software program version fissures that undermines CJTF tempo given current practices and policies. Players articulated that ships have limited bandwidth to share information. This limited bandwidth will limit the ability for the CJTF commander to quickly establish a COP, especially in the initial phases of the fight. Ensuring that limited bandwidth remains intact and that the enemy does not hamper the transmission of information or introduce malicious code into the CJTF network is critical to maintaining the flow of information. Finally, software programs may not be uniform across the CJTF. Players expressed frustration that mission tempo can easily be reduced by the need to convert between newer and older versions of software – like Microsoft Word.

There are potential capability and capacity shortfalls associated with moving and sustaining support for joint operational access operations.
Participants highlighted two capability shortfalls that would enable greater freedom of action in the EW12 scenario, mine-countermine (MCM) assets and theater ballistic missile defense (TBMD). For MCM capabilities, players were undecided on whether the operational gap was the numbers of platforms (as in inventory) or naval mine ISR in order to track mine-loading and distribution. A responsive missile defense capability was critical to setting the conditions necessary to maintaining freedom of action in an A2/AD environment. The task force relied on coverage from Aegis ships for both the seabase and the lodgment in the Savanna Islands, prior to the establishment of Army Patriot and THAAD batteries.

The naval force's lack of capacity – mostly as a product of lift limitations – increases the force's risk and vulnerabilities by potentially providing the adversary time to react to friendly force deployments. This lack of capacity manifests itself in finite shipboard space to embark troops and equipment, as well as the limited number of amphibious ships to execute operations simultaneously, vice sequentially. The increased deployment timelines potentially impact the CJTF's ability to gain the initiative, achieve surprise and control the operational tempo.

Surface connectors were another capability that was identified to have a capacity shortfall. Surface connectors that could transport troops and materiel from ship to shore would be in simultaneous demand by amphibious, Maritime Prepositioning Force (MPF) and Joint Logistics Over-the-Shore (JLOTS) operations. Landing craft air cushion (LCACs) and ship-to-shore connectors (SSCs) are fast but expensive, making it unlikely that the force will have them in the numbers required. Landing craft, utility (LCUs) are slow but have a large carrying capacity. Landing craft, mechanized (LCM-8s, or "Mike Boats") are both slow and have limited capacity. These throughput concerns are magnified by how the landing force is configured to fight ashore. A vehicle-intensive force presumably has more overland mobility and reach, but it also imposes a greater sustainment tax. The development of increasingly heavy armored vehicles to provide overland mobility in Afghanistan and Iraq has compounded the issues regarding shipboard space and throughput from ship to shore.

EW12 discussions and technical briefs highlighted constraints on other enabling capabilities. Key enablers such as Navy beach groups (BEACHGRU), construction battalion (SeaBees) and cargo handlers are available in limited numbers and often in the reserve component, forcing key tasks to be performed sequentially and slowing operational tempo. The operation would also be limited by the capability for bulk fuel movement and distribution, especially for the large naval force depicted in EW12 that includes multiple ARG/MEUs, CSGs, a "reinforced" MPSRON and JLOTS assets.

> **Wargame participants wondered aloud, "Why did we take the Savanna Islands?"**

There would also be significant pressure to quickly establish the APODs and SPODs needed to meet future timelines per the CJTF Savanna CONOPS. EW12 players raised questions about the key enablers to run the APOD in the Savanna Islands. Participants disagreed on whether the CFMCC or CFLCC would be better suited to manage the APOD's C2; repair runways; establish infrastructure; store and distribute petroleum, oil and lubricants (POL); and provide force protection.

Seabasing could be a decisive capability that sustains operations ashore and afloat, but it comes with a cost. Traditional MPF offloads create the proverbial "iron mountain" ashore, which leaves a large footprint and is operationally impractical if commanders seek to access equipment or sustainment buried on the bottom decks of a maritime prepositioning ship. Seabasing seeks to diminish the ashore footprint and create more shipboard space for selective access, but this shifts the operational burden afloat and increases the force's overall fuel consumption.

Wargame participants wondered aloud, *"Why did we take the Savanna Islands?"* but there were few other realistic alternatives that could keep the force sustained. Thus, a naval expeditionary force that seeks bold maneuver to reach objectives – in the spirit of OMFTS/STOM – needed a lodgment to maintain tempo into the next phases of the operation. Players asserted that sustainment is the true measure of an "expeditionary" force. In EW12, CJTF Savanna had several operational-level challenges to sustaining its forces, including SOF's ability to tap into the GPF and host nation sustainment network, the CJTF's ability to sustain its non-U.S. allies, and cross-service coordination issues.

Cyber capabilities in 2024 will likely be significantly different than those of today. Policy, capability, and capacity issues related to cyber will require additional research.
Players expressed concern that current organization and command relationship structures do not adequately account for the integration of cyber elements into the CJTF. Organizationally, it was not clear how the CJTF might integrate cyber into its command structure. For example, do planning staffs incorporate cyber planners as non-kinetic fires advisors or do more effective organizational relationships exist? At the MAGTF level, there is also a lack of clarity regarding organizational and command relationship structures. Players expressed a strong desire to further examine how the CJTF commander can integrate cyberspace operations for effective employment in support of the CJTF's mission.

Some players also said that legal authorities or limitations may impact the ability of the CJTF in the application of cyber effects. However, EW12 players also pointed out that there may be other means to create the desired effect.   Currently, the CJTF commander lacks the authority to control the cyber domain in the battlespace. Coalition partners' authorities may allow them to deliver cyber effects in support of the CJTF that U.S. forces cannot. Policy needs to clarify if the CJTF commander can use these coalition assets, or if the coalition assets will have to integrate at the GCC or some other level of command.

Players identified the long-term nature of exploitation requirements in cyberspace as a potential driver that prevents the CJTF commander from having cyber authorities. Although players understood that these exploitation requirements existed, they also recognized the need to educate planning staffs on cyber weapons' capabilities. These staffs require the knowledge on how to use cyber weapons to achieve effects in support of the mission.

A cyber toolkit was one solution offered to provide planning staffs with the necessary familiarity of U.S. cyber capabilities. This toolkit could identify which cyber weapons the commander may be able to control versus those that it should not control. Players acknowledged that some cyber weapons may be "one-shot wonders," causing higher echelons of command to restrict the use of these weapons.

Players expressed a desire to examine cyber lexicon and education at the planning staff level. Questions arose as to whether or not fires terminology supported a greater or lesser understanding of cyber capabilities. It would be useful if planning staffs understood the types of missions U.S. cyber capabilities can support and how these weapons might achieve specific effects.

Planning staffs need to further educate themselves on the utility of exploitation versus attack. Players questioned if disabling the enemy cyber infrastructure would undermine elements of the larger CJTF mission. Operations, like deception, may require the commander to ensure that the enemy can see, sense and respond to the movements of coalition forces. There is also a need to develop a structured review process that enables planning staffs to measure the effectiveness of cyber weapons used in support of the CJTF. Finally, there is a recognition that cyber capabilities in the 2024 environment, and perhaps the authorities associated with their employment, could be significantly different than today.

Key Insights and Recommendations

This section captures insights and recommended actions following extensive analysis of EW12 game design, execution, discussions and feedback from senior leaders. Some of these insights and actions reinforce ongoing joint, naval and Service initiatives, while others reflect new lessons learned that merit further exploration.

Command Arrangements

Modern threats call for the integrated application of naval capabilities throughout the maritime domain, but Navy and Marine Corps capabilities and expertise are largely focused seaward or landward, respectively, rather than holistically focused on the domain as a whole. We do not have adequate doctrine for aggregation of naval forces necessary for littoral and crisis response operations. Command elements are optimized for execution of Service versus "naval" operations. Command arrangement solutions are constrained by finite space and bandwidth afloat.

EW12 observations and insights reinforced solutions already in progress to address these issues. The most prominent of these is the Naval Services Game 2012 (NSG12), a joint Navy-

Marine Corps wargame approved by the Naval Board in March 2012 that will explore force aggregation. This initiative, led by the wargaming organizations of both Services, will take place on 11-13 September 2012 at the Naval War College in Newport, Rhode Island. New prospective tasks as a result of EW12 insights:

- DC CD&I G-3/G-5, coordinate with the Commander, Navy Warfare Development Command (CDR NWDC), to draft a proposal to the Naval Board for development of a concept for naval command arrangements.
  - Proposal due: 4th quarter, FY12
  - Concept prospectus submitted to Naval Board: 1st quarter, FY13
  - Concept published: End of FY13
- Commanding General, Training and Education Command (CG TECOM), coordinate with the Commander, Naval Education and Training Command (CDR NETC), to draft a proposal to the Naval Board for the establishment of a Naval Staff Training Program (NSTP) for Navy and Marine Corps officers.
  - Proposal due: 4th quarter, FY12
  - First NSTP exercise: 2nd quarter, FY14
- CG TECOM, coordinate with NETC, to draft a proposal to the Naval Board for assessment and potential refinements to Navy and Marine Corps PME.
  - Proposal due: 4th quarter, FY12
  - Assessment/recommendations published: 3rd quarter, FY13
- Deputy Commandant, Manpower and Reserve Affairs (DC M&RA), in coordination with the Chief of Naval Personnel, draft a proposal to the Naval Board for assessment and potential refinements to Navy and Marine Corps manpower and personnel policies that better integrate naval staffs in the fleets and operating forces.
  - Proposal due: 4th quarter, FY12
  - Assessment/recommendations published: 3rd quarter, FY13

Interoperability among Navy, Marine Corps, and SOF Capabilities

The Navy, Marine Corps and SOF possess many complementary capabilities that need better synchronization for the threats the joint force will face in the 21st century operating environment. An opportunity exists to enable force integration, formalize interoperability that enables naval forces and SOF to integrate when required by the mission, and better transition responsibilities from SOF to GPF in performing stability operations with host nation security forces.

A number of actions are already ongoing that will support the interoperability effort, which is being led by the Ellis Group, which evolved into a standing organization as a result of the

ACWG's mandate to review the strategic role, operating concepts and naval integration of the Marine Corps and the amphibious force. First is an initiative to create a multi-service concept that will define how USSOCOM and the naval services – the Navy, Marine Corps and Coast Guard – can coordinate and mutually support the conduct of forward engagement, crisis response, preparation of the environment, distributed operations, and combat operations. Second is a revitalization of the Marine Corps-USSOCOM Warfighter Talks, which have not occurred since 2009. Finally, there are ongoing efforts to improve naval and SOF training, education, and C2 to emphasize the ability of the forces to and complement each other's capabilities.

Initial EW12 insights reinforced many of the above activities, with subsequent follow-on actions fitting under one of the following four broad tasks:[14]

- Director, Strategic Initiatives Group, coordinate with Director, Public Affairs Division, to create external awareness of Marine Corps capabilities via strategic communications across the GCCs, joint community and naval services.
  - o Proposal due: Activities ongoing.
- CG TECOM, coordinate with Director, USSOCOM J-7/J-9 Knowledge, Training and Futures, to ensure Marine Corps training and education programs facilitate awareness of SOF capabilities and points of interoperability and integration.
  - o Proposal due: Activities ongoing.
- DC CD&I/Ellis Group, coordinate with relevant USSOCOM organizations, to formalize interoperability between the naval services and SOF that enables force integration when needed through a multi-service concept for engagement and stability operations.
  - o Proposal due: Activities ongoing.
- DC PP&O, coordinate with USSOCOM J-3/J-5, to demonstrate institutional commitment via formal mechanisms such as annual USMC-USSOCOM Warfighter Talks.
  - o Proposal due: Activities ongoing.

Information Sharing

EW12 showcased a number of common themes in doctrine, concepts and capabilities. Wargame attendees exposed seams in policy, practices and capabilities for optimal information management. They pointed out that the sharing of information is a "wicked problem" that cuts across a number of different dichotomies – U.S. and coalition, coalition and host nation, joint

---

[14] Discussions between the Marine Corps and USSOCOM regarding the *Multi-Service Concept for Distributed Engagement and Crisis Response in the Maritime Environment* have continued through summer 2012. A comprehensive list of tasks to strengthen interoperability and integration was scheduled to be published by August 2012.

and Service, GPF and SOF. HQMC/C4 is involved in DOD Focus Teams and Service working groups that are attempting to frame the problem. The following task outlines follow-on action by relevant stakeholders:

- Director, HQMC C4, participate in ongoing DOD-wide focus groups and activities that (1) identify policies that preclude the sharing of data and information; (2) identify a common set of data standards that enables multiple systems to present information that can be acted upon; (3) identify the presentation of actionable information that is derived from multiple data feeds in an effort to mitigate the impacts of information overload; and (4) socialize EW12 "information sharing" dilemmas with the Services, DOD entities and other federal agencies that are attempting to address this problem.
  - Proposal due: Activities ongoing.

Capacity Limitations

The wargame exposed numerous disconnects and shortfalls in capabilities and capacities that may hamper tempo and maneuver in a dynamic A2/AD environment. Some of these were related to countering A2/AD threats such as mine-clearing capabilities and readily available TBMD assets. Players discussed capacity shortfalls such as ship-to-shore connectors, APOD/SPOD support personnel, and construction capabilities to establish the lodgment required by the CJTF Savanna CONOPS.

Wargame participants noted that establishment of the lodgment was essential for the introduction of joint and naval forces into the JOA. However, requirements to establish a lodgment in an A2/AD environment will restrict maneuver and reduce the rate of force closure, impacting operational tempo. EW12 was not able to fully examine the capacity issues associated with building that lodgment. Prepositioning SMEs also observed that current policy and doctrine governing force development planning and execution (FDP&E) assumes that the A2/AD threat has been defeated. MPSRONs, which would provide a bulk of the follow-on forces for the scenario illustrated during EW12, will not operate in a semi-permissive environment.

Because the Marine Corps is dependent on Navy enablers to introduce and sustain a combat force in a maritime environment, a holistic understanding of current capabilities and readiness can help define where capacity ends. This has a intuitive tie-in with an ongoing effort led by DC PP&O (Readiness Section, POR) to understand and assess how the readiness of Navy forces impacts the Marine Corps' ability to execute joint operations in the maritime domain.

The above discussion prompted these recommended actions to address the capacity limitations highlighted during the wargame:

- COMMARFORs, coordinate with relevant NAVFORs, to establish a plan to better leverage MCM capabilities from coalition partners and host nation security forces in the conduct of A2/AD operations.
  - Proposal due: Activities ongoing.
- DC CD&I, coordinate with COMMARFORCOM, to ensure that FDP&E requirements to close a force in an A2/AD environment are assessed in future wargames.
  - Proposal due: Activities ongoing.
- DC PP&O, coordinate with Commander, Military Sealift Command and OPNAV N43, to develop a process for recurring readiness assessment of Navy enablers (e.g., Navy prepositioning enablers and ARGs).
  - Proposal due: 2nd quarter, FY13
- DC CD&I – coordinate with DC PP&O, DC I&L, OPNAV N42, OPNAV N81 and Commander, MSC – to develop an integrated, cohesive seabasing doctrine that considers the roles and responsibilities of MPF, JLOTS, seabasing, and other Services' afloat prepositioning capabilities (e.g., afloat Army Prepositioning Stocks (APS), the Combat Logistics Force (CLF) and Air Force afloat prepositioning).
  - Proposal due: 2nd quarter, FY13

Non-Kinetic Effects

The future plans and operations organizations – as currently defined, staffed and executed – do not fully incorporate available non-kinetic capabilities. This is due to insufficient non-kinetic subject matter expertise within the MAGTF initial OPT, future plans and future operations. In general, leaders and planners possess insufficient knowledge of relative strengths and limitations of non-kinetic capabilities in their ability to affect operational conditions.

Additionally, EW12 players and cyber SMEs observed that use of the decide, detect, deliver and assess (D3A) targeting process as a primary integration method for non-kinetic capabilities (like cyberspace operations) is sub-optimal because of the operational nature of most non-kinetic capabilities. Integration is critically dependent upon the ability of commanders and planners to understand non-kinetic capabilities and to sew them directly into the fabric of operational design, the CONOPS and the scheme of maneuver. EW12 participants said achieving this will lead to more natural integration of fires, maneuver and non-kinetic capabilities during execution.

During the wargame, gaps in the integration of electronic warfare into the MAGTF construct also were exposed. The MAGTF Electronic Warfare Concept of Operations calls for increased electromagnetic spectrum (EMS) effects through the integration of capabilities and capacities of all EMS-reliant functionalities. The Marine Corps, in conjunction with the joint force, must be able to control the EMS in order to exploit it.

The ability to dynamically assess the environment and task assets constitutes maneuver within the spectrum and ensures an offensive posture with requisite defensive readiness. The joint force must continue development of options for increasing Marine Corps EMS capability and capacity, which will be achieved through education, MOS development and staffing, and the fielding of dynamic electronic warfare capabilities and associated architectures.

Among the solutions already in development to address cyber integration are the Marine Corps Force Structure Review Group's (FSRG) recommendation to add cyber specialists to the Total Force (FY12-16), including the addition of a direct support company to supplement MAGTF operations, the maturation of the Electronic Warfare Coordination Center as an operational-level coordination hub for deployed MAGTFs, and education and training solutions identified in the Cyberspace Operations Initial Capabilities Document (ICD).

An EW12 cyberspace capabilities working group recommended the following additional solutions to address cyber-related issues highlighted during the wargame:

- DC CD&I, coordinate in coordination with COMMARFORCYBER, DC PP&O, CG TECOM and Director HQMC/C4, to develop a Service concept for combined arms and capabilities integration. This concept should explain a process for integrated and continuous planning and execution that places as much emphasis on integrating capabilities into future/deep operations as current/close operations. The concept should provide a framework within which fires, maneuver and support elements, and non-kinetic capabilities are planned and integrated into the MAGTF CONOPS and scheme of maneuver.
    - Proposal due: 1st quarter, FY13
- DC CD&I, coordinate with DC Aviation, Director, HQMC Intelligence Department, DC PP&O, CDR NAVAIRSYSCOM, COMMARCORSYSCOM, COMMARFORCYBER, COMMARFORCOM, COMMARFORPAC, and CG TECOM, to develop the following capabilities in accordance with the MAGTF Electronic Warfare Concept: (1) Electronic Warfare Services Architecture; (2) Unmanned Aerial System Spectrum Warfare Payloads; (3) Tactical Air Spectrum Warfare Payloads; (4) Vehicle and Manpack

Spectrum Warfare Kits; (5) A professional EMS warfare community and organization; and (6) an Electronic Warfare Coordination Cell.
- o Proposal due: Activities ongoing.
- o Expected Initial Operating Capability: FY17

Way Ahead

EW12 observations and discussions were presented to about 120 executive-level representatives from the U.S. and coalition defense community at the EW12 Executive Outbrief on 23 March 2012 at National Defense University. The Post-Game Workshop, held on 24 April 2012 at MCB Quantico, sought to synthesize the gaps and opportunities identified at the wargame to begin the process of analyzing discussions, refining the outputs and transitioning them for action. In turn, these actions will inform a number of approaching experiments, exercises and wargames.

- In the 3rd quarter of FY13, the Marine Corps Warfighting Laboratory will conduct **Enhanced MAGTF Operations Limited Objective Experiment 3 (EMO LOE-3) during Exercise Dawn Blitz 2013 (DB13) in June 2013 off the coast of Southern California**. The LOE will focus on MAGTF fires processes, but this MEB-level amphibious exercise also seeks to execute many of the concepts outlined during EW12. DB13 exercise objectives that focus on current capabilities include:
  - o Deep penetration with airlifted forces into the Marine Corps Air-Ground Combat Center at Twentynine Palms.
  - o Amphibious operations with reduced logistics and combat support buildup ashore.
  - o Counter-A2/AD threat operations and establish sea control.
  - o Over-the-horizon operations with available connectors.
- The topic of **NSG12 in September 2012** will be force aggregation. The game design was in development as of the drafting of this report, but the objective of the game is to develop principles and identify potential gaps that result from the aggregation of naval forces beyond the ARG/MEU and CSG.
- The Marine Corps' next Title 10 wargame, **EW13 scheduled for winter 2013 in the National Capital Region**, will explore Future Maritime Operations (FMO), a nascent concept that assesses requirements of naval forces in 2035.
- **EMO Advanced Warfighting Experiment (AWE) will be integrated with Exercise Rim of the Pacific 2014 (RIMPAC 14), scheduled for the 4th quarter of FY14 in Hawaii**. The exercise will be characterized by a deployable MEB command element, as well as

multiple, concurrent and distributed company landing teams conducting STOM and supported from the seabase.

Conclusion

EW12 exposed numerous gaps and opportunities in doctrine, concepts, capabilities and capacity for joint force operations in an A2/AD environment. In many cases, the potential solutions are as complex as the problems themselves, involving myriad organizations that must coordinate and integrate their respective capabilities to create unity of effort within the current and future operating environment. The Marine Corps' efforts to assess its expeditionary capabilities, as well as its partnership with the Navy, reflect a golden opportunity to shape the Service into the responsive, agile and lethal force envisioned in OMFTS and STOM. This is the first step forward.

MCWL Wargaming Contact Information

- Director, Dr. William Lademan, (703) 784-1035, william.lademan@usmc.mil

- Deputy Director, Col Tom Connally, (703) 784-3278, thomas.j.connally@usmc.mil

- EW Action Officer, Mr. Jeff Wong, (703) 784-6884, jeffrey.w.wong.ctr@usmc.mil

- Wargaming Division Administrative Office, (703) 784-3276, EW@usmc.mil

- Expeditionary Warrior 2012 Web Site:
  http://www.marines.mil/unit/mcwl/wargaming/ew/Pages/index.aspx

Appendix A: EW12 Participating Organizations

Department of Defense

- U.S. Marine Corps
  - Headquarters Marine Corps
    - AVN
    - C4
    - CD&I / MCCDC
    - Expeditionary Energy
    - I&L
    - PP&O
    - P&R
  - MARFORCOM
    - II MEF
    - 26 MEU
  - MARFORPAC
    - I MEF
    - 13 MEU
  - MARSOC
  - MARFORCYBER
  - MCIA
  - MCIOC
  - MCWAR
  - MCWL
- U.S. Navy
  - CPR-4
  - NAMDC
  - NBG-2
  - NECC
  - NWDC
  - Office of Naval Research
  - OPNAV (N42, N53, N85)
  - Strike Fighter Wing Atlantic
  - U.S. Fleet Forces Command
- U.S. Army
  - ARCIC
  - CASCOM
  - HQDA G-4
  - SMDC/ARSTRAT

- U.S. Air Force
  - Headquarters Air Force
    - A5XS
    - A8XC
- U.S. Coast Guard
  - CG-532
- U.S. Central Command
- U.S. Special Operations Command
  - J-7/J-9
- Joint Staff
  - J-4
  - J-7, Joint and Coalition Warfighting
- Military Sealift Command
- Office of the Secretary of Defense

U.S. Department of State

- Bureau of Conflict and Stabilization Operations

Multinational Partners

- Australia
- Brazil
- Canada
- Denmark
- Finland
- France
- Germany
- Italy
- Japan
- Netherlands
- Singapore
- South Korea
- Spain
- United Kingdom

Appendix B: Acronyms

A2/AD	Anti-Access/Area Denial
AADC	Area Air Defense Commander
AAW	Antiair Warfare
ACE	Aviation Combat Element
ACWG	Amphibious Capabilities Working Group
AOA	Amphibious Objective Area
AOR	Area of Responsibility
APOD	Air Point of Debarkation
ARG	Amphibious Ready Group
ASB	Air-Sea Battle
ATF	Amphibious Task Force
C4	Command, Control, Communications and Computers Division
CATF	Commander, Amphibious Task Force
CD&I	Combat Development and Integration
CE	Command Element
CEC	Cooperative Engagement Capability
CFACC	Combined Forces Air Component Commander
CFLCC	Combined Forces Land Component Commander
CFMCC	Combined Forces Maritime Component Commander
CJTF	Combined Joint Task Force
CLF	Commander, Landing Force or Combat Logistics Force
CMC	Commandant of the Marine Corps
CNO	Chief of Naval Operations
COP	Common Operating Picture
CSG	Carrier Strike Group
CWC	Composite Warfare Commander
EW	Expeditionary Warrior or Electronic Warfare
FFCC	Force Fires Coordination Center
G-RAMM	Guided Rockets, Artillery, Missiles and Mortars
GCC	Geographic Combatant Commander
GCE	Ground Combat Element
HIDACZ	High-Density Aircraft Control Zone
ISR	Intelligence, Surveillance and Reconnaissance
JLOTS	Joint Logistics Over the Shore
JOA	Joint Operations Area
JOAC	Joint Operational Access Concept
LCE	Logistics Combat Element

LCS	Littoral Combat Ship
LF	Landing Force
MAGTF	Marine Air-Ground Task Force
MARSOC	Marine Corps Forces Special Operations Command
MCCDC	Marine Corps Combat Development Command
MCWL	Marine Corps Warfighting Laboratory
MEB	Marine Expeditionary Brigade
MEF	Marine Expeditionary Force
MEU	Marine Expeditionary Unit
MOC	Maritime Operations Center
MPF	Maritime Prepositioning Force
MSC	Military Sealift Command
NWDC	Navy Warfare Development Command
OMFTS	Operational Maneuver from the Sea
SNB	Single Naval Battle
SOCOM	Special Operations Command
SOF	Special Operations Forces
SPOD	Sea Point of Debarkation
STOM	Ship-to-Objective Maneuver
TACC	Tactical Air Control Center
THAAD	Terminal High-Altitude Air Defense

Appendix C: EW12 Research Questions

The following research questions were developed to focus cell discussions on pertinent issues related to the game objective, sub-objectives and focus areas.

Vignette 1: Savanna Islands Anti-Access

Question #1 - How do the CFMCC lead elements (CSG and ARG/MEU) accomplish operations in an anti-access environment? Do they have sufficient capabilities? Are there solutions or resources that exist now, or will exist in the future, to address the capability issues? Are there alternatives for maneuver that circumvent anti-access threats?

Question #2 - What critical capabilities are required within and in support of CFMCC lead elements to maintain expeditionary missile defense to counter conventional anti-access?

Question #3 - In an anti-access environment, what Service doctrinal issues must be overcome to support force aggregation of CFMCC lead elements? What doctrinal issues must be overcome for the CFMCC to generate greater mutual support with the joint force (e.g., combat search and rescue, unmanned aerial systems and TBMD)?

Vignette #2: SOF and CFMCC Interoperability

Question #4 - What conditions can be set by the CFMCC in support of CFSOCC operations? How can CFMCC leverage support from CFSOCC operations? How will conditions within the littorals be set? What SOF capabilities / augmentation / liaison are needed within CFMCC lead elements? How does the TSOC factor into CFSOCC operations and interoperability with the CFMCC? Can the CFMCC assist in CFSOCC enable, support and sustainment (ESS) issues?

Question #5 - What are the organizational and doctrinal challenges to CFMCC/CFSOCC mission set synergy? What concepts should be developed and tested to support interoperability? What battlespace coordination/C2 relationships should be codified to facilitate interoperability?

Vignette #3: Area-Denial in Vicinity of Savanna Mainland

Question #6 - What WAF/FSM area-denial capabilities pose the greatest risk to mission accomplishment? What interoperability gaps exist in joint/Service capabilities to defeat these threats? How does the CFMCC maintain maritime superiority against a coordinated WAF attack (missile, FAC, UAS or ground) against the seabase and lodgment?

Question #7 - What are the critical counter-AD requirements the CFMCC must address near the joint lodgment? What opportunities exist for joint contributions to maintain sea/air dominance at a joint lodgment? What are the key joint force vulnerabilities (e.g., offshore petroleum distribution system (OPDS) is immobile)? What elements of the littoral movement profile (e.g., LCAC, SURC, ACV, MV-22, etc.) support maritime superiority as an additional mission?

Question #8 - What doctrinal changes need to occur if the MAGTF C2 remains afloat or seabased? With MAGTF aviation remaining afloat, what are the impacts on the coordination of airspace and fires if MAGTF C2 transitions ashore?

Vignette #4: Joint Lodgment

Question #9 - What are the throughput challenges for the joint force and the seabase if the joint lodgment is more austere and all logistics have to come over the shore?

Question #10 - What are critical throughput capabilities the CFMCC must maintain near the joint lodgment? What capabilities should be included with CFMCC lead elements and the seabase operating in a time-constrained operation?

Question #11 - How can the joint force better leverage the seabase's capabilities in light of future common airframes? What elements of the littoral movement profile (e.g., LCAC, LCU, LSV and JHSV) can be better leveraged to overcome interoperability challenges?

Question #12 - What are the critical requirements the seabase must provide to expand airfields for joint operations? How do these requirements impact aviation deployment concepts?

Vignette #5: CFMCC Support to Follow-on Operations

Question #13 - In this vignette, CFMCC retains control of landward battlespace. How will the MOC control operations in the landward battlespace? What are the doctrinal implications if CFLCC controls the landward battlespace within the littoral?

Question #14 - Does strict adherence to functional componency and the geographic domains inhibit joint operations in the littorals? Does current amphibious doctrine meet the needs of littoral operations (AOA/HIDACZ)? How do we resolve these issues?

Question #15 - What are the perceived gaps developing in amphibious doctrine when unmanned air, sea and sub-surface systems are considered to be operating from multiple services in the close-in littorals?